SIMONE MANUEL

BY MATT SCHEFF

SportsZone

An Imprint of Abdo Publishing
abdopublishing.com

abdopublishing.com

Published by Abdo Publishing, a division of ABDO, PO Box 398166, Minneapolis, Minnesota 55439. Copyright © 2017 by Abdo Consulting Group, Inc. International copyrights reserved in all countries. No part of this book may be reproduced in any form without written permission from the publisher. SportsZone™ is a trademark and logo of Abdo Publishing.

Printed in the United States of America, North Mankato, Minnesota
102016
012017

Cover Photo: Lee Jin-man/AP Images
Interior Photos: Martin Meissner/AP Images, 4-5, 22-23; Joel Marklund/ZumaPress/ Newscom, 6, 24-25; Sean Kilpatrick/The Canadian Press/AP Images, 7; Gabriel Bouys/ AFP/Getty Images, 8-9; Shutterstock Images, 10-11; Adam Pretty/Getty Images Sport/ Getty Images, 12, 13; Dai Sugano/Bay Area News Group/TNS/Newscom, 14-15, 16-17; Mark J. Terrill/AP Images, 18-19, 20, 21; Daniel A. Anderson/ZumaPress/Newscom, 26; Gary Hershorn/Silverhub/ZumaPress/Newscom, 27; Eric Christian Smith/AP Images, 28; Matt Patterson/AP Images, 29

Editor: Chrös McDougall
Series Designer: Jake Nordby

Publisher's Cataloging-in-Publication Data

Names: Scheff, Matt, author.
Title: Simone Manuel / by Matt Scheff.
Description: Minneapolis, MN : Abdo Publishing, 2017. | Series: Olympic stars |
    Includes bibliographical references and index.
Identifiers: LCCN 2016951818 | ISBN 9781680785609 (lib. bdg.) |
    ISBN 9781680785883 (ebook)
Subjects: LCSH: Manuel, Simone, 1996- --Juvenile literature. | Swimmers--
    United States--Biography--Juvenile literature. | Women Olympic athletes--
    United States--Biography--Juvenile literature. | Olympic Games (31st : 2016 :
    Rio de Janeiro, Brazil)
Classification: DDC 797.2/1092 [B]--dc23
LC record available at http://lccn.loc.gov/2016951818

CONTENTS

Simone Manuel dives in to start the 2016 Olympic 100-meter freestyle final.

HISTORIC CHAMPION

Simone Manuel had work to do. The 20-year-old swimmer was competing at the 2016 Olympic Games in Rio de Janeiro, Brazil. But midway through the 100-meter freestyle final, Manuel had fallen back to the middle of the pack. It was now or never for her to make a move.

Then it happened. Manuel surged as the other racers tired and slowed. With each stroke, she pulled closer and closer to the lead. Then, with a final burst, Manuel reached out and touched the wall. She looked up to the scoreboard. She had finished with the same time as Canada's Penny Oleksiak. It was a tie for the gold medal! And not only that, Manuel became the first African-American woman to win gold in an Olympic swimming event.

After the race, Manuel said she was thinking about African-American swimmers who came before her. "I hope that I can be an inspiration for others," she said.

Manuel, *bottom*, races toward the finish in the 100-meter freestyle.

Penny Oleksiak, *right*, and Manuel celebrate their shared victory.

FAST FACT
Manuel and Penny Oleksiak set an Olympic record with their 100-meter freestyle time of 52.70 seconds.

Simone and her mom hug at the 2016 Olympics.

MAKING WAVES

Simone Ashley Manuel was born on August 2, 1996, in Sugar Land, Texas. Both of her parents had been athletes. Her dad even played basketball in college. Simone's parents encouraged their children to be active in sports.

Simone's older brothers, Chris and Ryan, competed on a swimming team. She liked watching them swim. At age four she started swimming lessons. She was hooked. Simone was a natural in the water. By only the second day in lessons, she could swim across the pool.

FAST FACT
The Manuel family motto is "D.Y.B." It stands for "do your best."

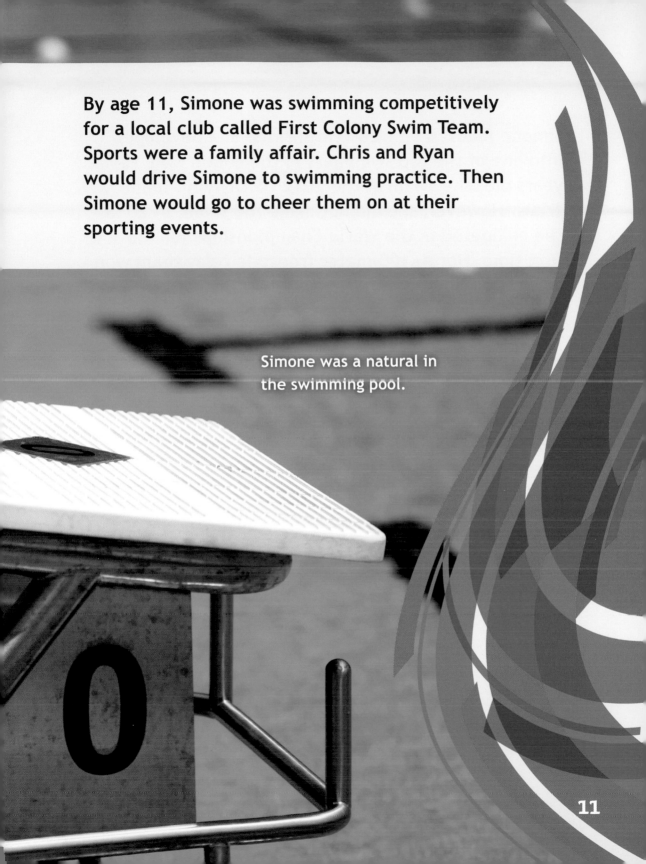

By age 11, Simone was swimming competitively for a local club called First Colony Swim Team. Sports were a family affair. Chris and Ryan would drive Simone to swimming practice. Then Simone would go to cheer them on at their sporting events.

Simone was a natural in the swimming pool.

Simone focused on freestyle sprints. She developed into one of the top swimmers in the country. At 15 years old, she swam at the 2012 US Olympic Team Trials. However, she did not make the team. In 2013 she competed in the World Championships for the first time. Her 4×100-meter freestyle relay team won gold. She also broke the 16-and-under record for the 50-meter freestyle.

Simone took her studies seriously. She graduated from Fort Bend Austin High School in 2014.

Simone races in the 4×100-meter freestyle relay at the 2013 World Championships.

Simone at the 2013
World Championships

FAST FACT
Simone's friends
gave her
the nickname
"Swimone."

TAKING THE NEXT STEP

In the fall of 2014, Manuel moved to California. She enrolled at Stanford University on a swimming scholarship. Manuel made an instant impact. As a freshman, she set the school records in the 50-, 100-, and 200-yard freestyle events.

"She's fearless," said competitor and fellow Team USA swimmer Missy Franklin.

FAST FACT

Manuel's brother Ryan played basketball for Southern Methodist University in Texas.

Manuel was a star from
the start at Stanford.

Manuel, *right*, and her Stanford teammate Lia Neal

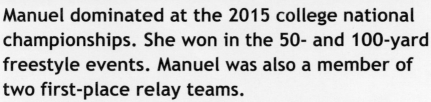

Manuel dominated at the 2015 college national championships. She won in the 50- and 100-yard freestyle events. Manuel was also a member of two first-place relay teams.

"She's capable of doing some pretty crazy things when she has an opportunity," said Stanford coach Greg Meehan.

FAST FACT
African-American swimmers took the top three spots in the 100-yard freestyle at the 2015 college national championships. That had never happened before. Manuel's teammate Lia Neal finished second.

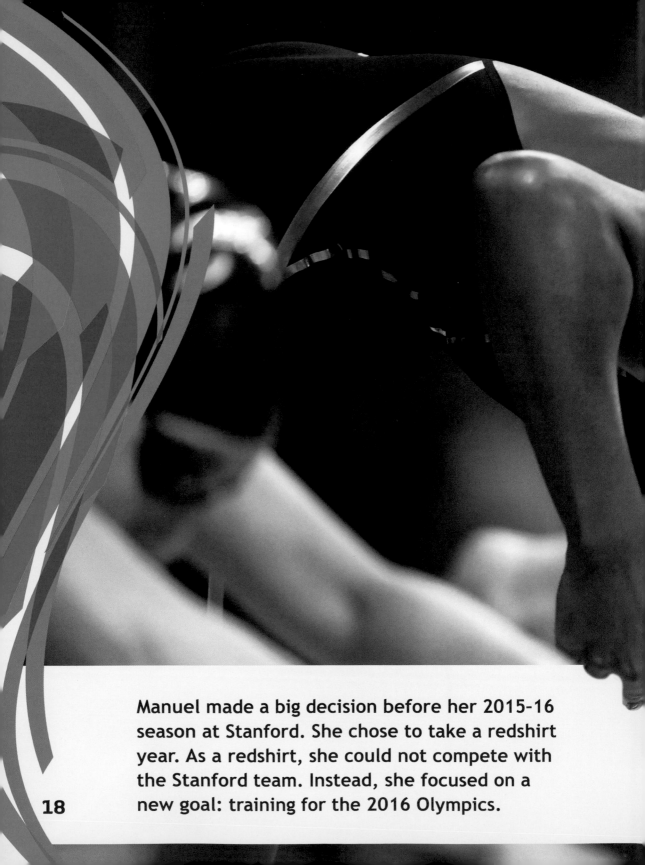

Manuel made a big decision before her 2015-16 season at Stanford. She chose to take a redshirt year. As a redshirt, she could not compete with the Stanford team. Instead, she focused on a new goal: training for the 2016 Olympics.

Manuel was ready when she got to the 2016 US Olympic Team Trials.

The 2016 US Olympic Team Trails were in Omaha, Nebraska. Manuel competed in three races. Only the top two finishers moved on to the Olympics. The United States had many great swimmers. Just making the Olympic team was a major challenge in some events. But Manuel made it! She finished second in the 50- and 100-meter freestyle races. Next up, it was off to Brazil for the Olympics.

Manuel, *left*, and Abbey Weitzeil start the 100-meter freestyle at the 2016 US Olympic Team Trials.

Manuel, *right*, and Abbey Weitzeil celebrate making the 2016 US Olympic Team in the 50-meter freestyle.

Manuel checks her time after a race at the 2016 Olympics.

FAST FACT
In 2000 Anthony Ervin became the first African-American swimmer to make the US Olympic Team.

GOING FOR GOLD

The pressure is high for all Olympians. But Manuel carried extra pressure with her. The United States had not produced many elite African-American swimmers. Manuel wanted to help change that.

"It seems cliché, but black people don't just jump in the pool," she said. "There's such a stereotype, and you don't see a lot of us swimming. I'm hoping to lead by example."

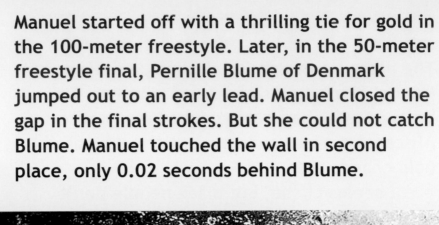

Manuel started off with a thrilling tie for gold in the 100-meter freestyle. Later, in the 50-meter freestyle final, Pernille Blume of Denmark jumped out to an early lead. Manuel closed the gap in the final strokes. But she could not catch Blume. Manuel touched the wall in second place, only 0.02 seconds behind Blume.

Manuel shows off her speed at the 2016 Olympics.

Next Manuel turned her attention to her relay races. She swam the anchor leg for the 4×100-meter medley relay team. Her teammates gave her a lead. Manuel held it every stroke of the way to the finish. Then she finished her Olympic Games by earning another silver medal with the 4×100-meter freestyle relay team.

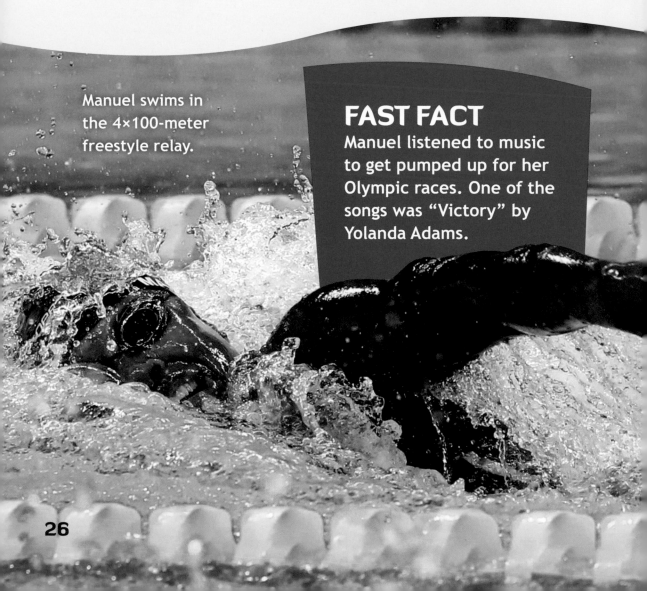

Manuel swims in the 4×100-meter freestyle relay.

FAST FACT
Manuel listened to music to get pumped up for her Olympic races. One of the songs was "Victory" by Yolanda Adams.

Manuel shows off one of her gold medals.

Manuel returned to the United States as a hero and a role model. Fans, dancers, and even a marching band flocked to the airport to welcome her home. Manuel soaked in the attention. But she did not have much time to rest. That fall she continued her college career at Stanford. Fans hope the best is yet to come.

Manuel lines up with the Houston Texans football team for the national anthem.

Manuel shows off her four Olympic medals at a Houston Texans game.

FAST FACT
The Houston Texans made Manuel a guest of honor at their preseason football game on August 28, 2016. She got to spend time on the field meeting some of the pro players.

TIMELINE

1996
Simone Ashley Manuel is born on August 2 in Sugar Land, Texas.

2007
Manuel swims for a local club, First Colony Swim Team.

2012
At age 15, Manuel swims at the US Olympic Team Trials, but she does not make the US team.

2013
Manuel wins the 4×100-meter freestyle relay gold medal at the World Championships. She also sets a new 16-and-under record for the 50-meter freestyle.

2014
Manuel graduates from high school and enrolls at Stanford University.

2015
Manuel wins the 50- and 100-yard freestyle events at the college national championships. She is also on two winning relay teams.

2015
Manuel competes in the World Championships and wins a bronze medal in the 4×100 freestyle relay.

2015
Manuel decides to take a redshirt season at Stanford so she can focus on the 2016 Olympics.

2016
Manuel wins four medals at the Olympics, including two golds. She becomes the first African-American woman to win Olympic gold in swimming.

GLOSSARY

anchor leg
The last of four sections in a relay race.

focus
To concentrate on and work toward a specific goal.

freestyle
A style of swimming in which swimmers can use any type of swimming stroke, although swimmers typically use the front crawl.

medley
A race that combines multiple kinds of strokes.

redshirt
When a college athlete can train with a team but not compete. The athlete does not use one of his or her four years of eligibility during a redshirt season.

relay
A race in which a team of four swimmers races one at a time.

scholarship
Money given to a student to help pay for school, usually because the student excels in a given area, such as in a sport.

sprint
A short, fast race.

stereotype
An oversimplified belief about someone or something.

surge
To suddenly move faster.

trials
An event that determines which athletes advance to a higher level of competition.

INDEX

About the Author

Matt Scheff is an artist and author living in Alaska. He enjoys mountain climbing, deep-sea fishing, and curling up with his two Siberian huskies to watch sports.